Freddie Freeman

The Baseball Kid

Who Never Gives Up

Benjamin Danielson

This book belongs to.........................

....

TABLE OF CONTENTS

INTRODUCTION

Freddie Freeman is a real-life baseball hero who shows us that with hard work and dedication, anything is possible.

Freddie is more than just a baseball player. He's a kind and generous person who loves to help others. He's also a great role model for kids, showing us the importance of hard work, perseverance, and believing in ourselves.

In this book, we'll take a journey through Freddie's life, from his early days as a baseball-loving kid to his incredible journey to becoming a World Series champion. We'll learn about his challenges, his triumphs, and the lessons he's learned along the way.

So, get ready to dive into the exciting world of baseball and discover the inspiring story of Freddie Freeman!

CHAPTER 1:

A BASEBALL-LOVING KID

A Baseball-Crazy Family

Freddie Freeman was born in Fountain Valley, California, a place where the sun always shines and the smell of freshly cut grass fills the air. From the moment he could walk, Freddie was drawn to baseball. His family was baseball crazy! His dad,

Fred, played baseball in college, and his mom, Lisa, was always cheering him on from the stands.

Every weekend, the Freeman family would head to the ballpark. The crack of the bat, the roar of the crowd, and the smell of hot dogs filled the air. Freddie loved every minute of it. He'd spend hours practicing in the backyard, pretending he was a famous baseball player.

"I've always loved baseball," Freddie would say. **"It's in my blood."**

As Freddie grew older, his love for baseball only grew stronger. He spent countless hours practicing, dreaming of one day playing in the major leagues.

Early Days on the Diamond

Freddie's first baseball team was the Fountain Valley Little League. He was a small kid, but he had a big heart and an even bigger love for the game. He'd spend hours practicing, working on his hitting, fielding, and pitching.

One day, during a Little League game, Freddie hit a home run. The ball soared over the fence, and the crowd erupted in cheers. Freddie was so excited! He'd never felt so proud. **"That was the best feeling in the world,"** he would later say.

As Freddie got older, he started playing on better and better teams. He was always one of the best players on the field, but he never let it go to his head. He was a humble kid who just loved to play baseball.

He'd spend countless hours in the batting cage, perfecting his swing. He'd practice fielding ground balls until his hands were raw. And he'd throw countless pitches, trying to develop his signature curveball.

Freddie's hard work and dedication paid off. He was soon recognized as one of the top young baseball players in the country. He was invited to play in prestigious tournaments and was often featured in baseball magazines.

Dreams of the Big Leagues

As Freddie grew older, his dreams of playing in the major leagues grew stronger. He would often stay up late at night, gazing at the stars and imagining himself standing on the field at Dodger Stadium, the roar of the crowd filling his ears.

He'd spend hours watching baseball games on TV, studying the moves of his favorite players. He'd practice their swings, their pitches, and their fielding techniques.

"I wanted to be just like them," Freddie would say. **"I wanted to be a baseball star."**

Freddie knew that the road to the major leagues would be long and difficult. He would have to work harder than ever before. But he was determined. He was ready to face any challenge, no matter how big.

He visualized himself hitting home runs, making diving catches, and pitching shutouts. He imagined the thrill of competing against the best players in the world. He dreamed of the day when he would be wearing a major league uniform, representing his team and his city.

With every swing of the bat and every toss of the ball, Freddie was one step closer to his dream. He knew that if he worked hard and never gave up, he could achieve anything he set his mind to.

CHAPTER 2:

THE HARD WORK BEGINS

Long Hours of Practice

To reach his dream of playing in the major leagues, Freddie knew he had to work harder than ever before. He spent countless hours practicing, day in and day out. The crack of the bat, the pop of the glove, and the hiss of the ball became the soundtrack of his life.

He'd wake up early in the morning, grab a quick breakfast, and head to the baseball field. He'd spend hours hitting balls, fielding grounders, and throwing pitches. The sun would beat down on him, but he never complained. He was determined to improve, to get better every day.

"Hard work is the key to success," Freddie often said. **"If you want to be the best, you have to outwork everyone else."**

He'd practice hitting until his arms ached, fielding ground balls until his hands were raw, and pitching until his shoulder felt like it was on fire. But he never gave up. He knew that every hour of practice brought him closer to his goal.

Learning from the Best

To become the best, Freddie knew he had to learn from the best. He watched videos of legendary players like Hank Aaron and Willie Mays, studying their every move. He tried to mimic their swings, their fielding techniques, and their baserunning.

Freddie also sought advice from experienced coaches and players. He listened carefully to their tips and tricks, and he applied them to his own game. He was always eager to learn, always striving to improve.

"The best players are always learning," Freddie would say. **"You can never stop improving."**

One of Freddie's biggest influences was his high school coach, Mike Devereaux, a former major league player. Devereaux taught Freddie the importance of discipline, hard work, and perseverance. He pushed Freddie to be the best he could be, both on and off the field.

With Devereaux's guidance, Freddie continued to develop his skills. He became a standout high school player, and his talent caught the attention of major league scouts.

Overcoming Challenges

Like any athlete, Freddie faced challenges along his journey. There were times when he struggled at the plate, his pitches weren't as sharp as usual, or injuries slowed him down. But he never let these setbacks discourage him.

He learned that failure is an inevitable part of the game. It's how you respond to failure that truly matters. Freddie would analyze his mistakes, work hard to correct them, and come back stronger than ever.

"You're going to have bad days," Freddie would say. **"The key is to learn from them and move on."**

One of the biggest challenges Freddie faced was the immense pressure to perform. As a highly-touted prospect, everyone had high expectations for him. But he handled the pressure with grace and maturity. He focused on his own game, blocked out the noise, and let his talent shine.

He also learned the importance of staying positive, even when things weren't going his way. He'd often remind himself of his goals and the hard work he'd put in to get to where he was. He knew that if he kept his head up and stayed focused, he would eventually overcome any obstacle.

Through it all, Freddie's unwavering belief in himself and his relentless work ethic helped him navigate the challenges and emerge as a true champion.

CHAPTER 3:

RISING STAR

A Promising Young Player

As a high school senior, Freddie was already being touted as one of the top baseball prospects in the country. His talent was undeniable, and major league scouts were eager to see him play.

On draft day, Freddie sat with his family, nervously awaiting his name to be called. When the Atlanta Braves selected him with the second overall pick, the room erupted in cheers. It was a dream come true!

"I was so excited," Freddie recalled. **"To be drafted by the Braves was a dream come true."**

Freddie quickly made his way through the minor league system, impressing everyone with his hitting, fielding, and leadership skills. He was known for his strong work ethic, his positive attitude, and his ability to perform under pressure.

He dominated at every level, hitting home runs, driving in runs, and playing stellar defense. His talent was undeniable, and it was clear that he was destined for greatness.

As Freddie climbed the minor league ladder, he faced new challenges and opportunities. He learned to adapt to different pitching styles, different playing fields, and different pressures. But through it all, he remained focused and determined. He knew that with hard work and dedication, he could achieve his dreams.

Making His Major League Debut

The day finally arrived. After years of hard work and dedication, Freddie Freeman was ready to make his major league debut. He put on his Atlanta Braves uniform, feeling a mix of excitement and nervousness.

As he stepped onto the field, the roar of the crowd filled his ears. The lights were bright, the air was electric, and the moment was unforgettable.

"It was a dream come true," Freddie later said. **"To be playing in the major leagues was something I had always wanted."**

In his first at-bat, Freddie stepped up to the plate, took a deep breath, and swung. The crowd held its breath as the ball soared through the air. It landed safely in the outfield, and

Freddie sprinted to first base, sliding into the bag. The crowd erupted in cheers.

From that moment on, Freddie was a force to be reckoned with. He quickly established himself as one of the best young players in baseball. He was a gifted hitter, a skilled defender, and a natural leader.

A Breakout Season

In 2013, Freddie had a breakout season. He hit home runs, drove in runs, and played excellent defense. He was a key player on a Braves team that made a deep playoff run.

One of the highlights of his season was a dramatic home run he hit in the playoffs. The ball soared over the fence, and the crowd went wild. It was a moment that Freddie would never forget.

"That was one of the best moments of my career," he said. **"To hit a home run in the playoffs was a dream come true."**

Freddie's performance that season earned him the National League MVP award. He was just 23 years old, and he was already one of the best players in baseball.

CHAPTER 4:

A WORLD SERIES

CHAMPION

The Road to the World Series

The 2021 season was a special one for Freddie and the Atlanta Braves. They faced many challenges, but they never gave up. They fought hard every game, and their determination paid off.

The Braves clinched the National League East division title, securing a spot in the playoffs. They then battled through the playoffs, defeating tough opponents like the Milwaukee Brewers and the Los Angeles Dodgers.

"It was a thrilling ride," Freddie said. **"We never stopped believing in ourselves."**

Freddie was a key player in the Braves' playoff run. He hit clutch home runs, drove in runs, and played stellar defense. His leadership and positive attitude inspired his teammates.

A Thrilling Championship Run

The World Series was a thrilling series, filled with dramatic moments and unforgettable plays. The Braves faced the Houston Astros, a tough and talented team.

One of the most exciting moments of the series was when Freddie hit a clutch home run to help the Braves win a crucial game. The crowd erupted in cheers, and the Braves dugout erupted in celebration.

"It was a feeling like no other," Freddie said. **"To hit a home run in the World Series was a dream come true."**

The Braves and Astros battled back and forth, trading wins and losses. The series went all the way to Game

6, where the Braves emerged victorious.

As the final out was recorded, the Braves players and fans erupted in joy. They had done it! They had won the World Series! Freddie had finally achieved his lifelong dream.

Celebrating Victory

The celebration after the World Series win was unforgettable. The Braves players and fans poured onto the field, hugging, cheering, and spraying champagne. It was a night of pure joy and excitement.

Freddie was overjoyed. He had worked so hard for this moment, and now it was finally here. He had achieved his lifelong dream of becoming a World Series champion.

"It's a feeling I'll never forget," Freddie said. **"To share this moment with my teammates and fans was incredible."**

The parade through the streets of Atlanta was a sight to behold. Fans lined the streets, cheering and waving flags. The energy was electric, and the city was buzzing with excitement.

Freddie rode in the parade, soaking up the love and admiration of the fans. It was a moment of pure joy and gratitude.

The World Series victory was a testament to Freddie's hard work, dedication, and perseverance. He had overcome challenges, faced adversity, and emerged as a true

champion.

CHAPTER 5:

A ROLE MODEL FOR KIDS

The Importance of Hard Work

Freddie Freeman is more than just a baseball player; he's a role model for kids everywhere. He teaches us the importance of hard work, dedication, and perseverance.

"Hard work is the key to success," Freddie often says. "If you want to achieve your dreams, you have to put in the work."

Freddie didn't become a World Series champion overnight. It took years of hard work and dedication. He spent countless hours practicing, pushing himself to be better. He never gave up, even when things got tough.

"You're going to face challenges," Freddie says. **"But it's how you respond to those challenges that defines you."**

Freddie's story inspires us to never give up on our dreams. No matter how big or small your dream may be, if you work hard and believe in yourself, you can achieve it.

The Power of Perseverance

One of the most important qualities Freddie possesses is perseverance. This means he never gives up, even when things get tough. He keeps trying, even when it seems impossible.

Freddie has faced many challenges throughout his career. He's had to overcome injuries, slumps, and the pressure of expectations. But he's always bounced back stronger than before.

"It's important to never give up on your dreams," Freddie says. **"Keep working hard, and eventually, you'll achieve your goals."**

Perseverance is a powerful tool that can help you overcome any obstacle. It's the key to success in all areas of life, not just sports. So the next time you face a challenge, remember Freddie's story and keep pushing forward.

Giving Back to the Community

Freddie Freeman is not only a talented baseball player, but he's also a kind and generous person. He believes in giving back to the community and helping others.

He and his wife, Chelsea, have started a foundation to help children in need. They support various charities and organizations, and they often volunteer their time to help others.

"It's important to use your platform to make a positive impact," Freddie says. **"We're**

blessed to be in a position to help others, and we're grateful for the opportunity."

Freddie's commitment to giving back is an inspiration to us all. He shows us that we can use our talents and resources to make a difference in the world.

LESSONS AND

MESSAGE FOR KIDS

Freddie Freeman's story teaches us many valuable lessons. He shows us that with hard work, dedication, and perseverance, we can achieve our dreams.

He also teaches us the importance of staying positive, even when things get tough. A positive attitude can help us overcome challenges and reach our goals.

Freddie's message to kids is simple: **"Believe in yourself, work hard, and never give up."**

If you have a dream, chase it. Don't let anyone tell you it's impossible. With hard work and dedication, you can achieve anything. Remember, the only limit is your imagination.

FUN FACTS ABOUT

FREDDIE FREEMAN

1. **Baseball-Loving Family:** Freddie comes from a baseball-loving family. His dad, Fred, played baseball in college!

2. **Early Baseball Days:** Freddie started playing baseball when he was just a little kid. He loved spending time on the field, practicing and playing games.

3. **A Big Eater:** Freddie loves to eat! He's known for his big appetite and his love for good food.

4. **A Dog Lover:** Freddie has a cute dog named Cooper. They often spend time together, playing fetch and going for walks.

5. **A World Series Champion:** Freddie is a World Series champion! He helped the Atlanta

Braves win the World Series in 2021.

6. **A Great Hitter:** Freddie is one of the best hitters in baseball. He can hit the ball really hard and far!

7. **A Good Teammate:** Freddie is a great teammate. He's always encouraging his teammates and helping them out.

8. **A Role Model:** Freddie is a role model for kids. He shows us the

importance of hard work, dedication, and perseverance.

FREDDIE FREEMAN

QUOTES FOR KIDS

Here are some inspiring quotes from Freddie Freeman, explained in a way kids can understand:

"Hard work is the key to success."

This means that if you want to be good at something, you have to practice a lot.

"Never give up on your dreams."

Even if things get tough, keep trying your best. Don't give up on what you want to achieve.

"Believe in yourself."

You should always think you can do it. Believe in your own abilities.

"The only limit is your imagination."

You can dream big and aim high. There's no limit to what you can achieve.

"It's important to use your platform to make a positive impact."

When you're famous, you can help others. Freddie uses his fame to help people in need.

A TIMELINE OF LIFE

AND CAREER

Early Life and Career:

- **1989:** Born in Villa Park, California.

- **2007:** Drafted by the Atlanta Braves in the second round of the MLB draft.

- **2010:** Made his MLB debut with the Atlanta Braves.

Rise to Stardom:

- **2013**: Earned his first All-Star selection and won the Silver Slugger Award.

- **2018**: Won his first Gold Glove Award.

- **2020**: Won the National League MVP Award.

World Series Champion:

- **2021:** Won his first World Series championship with the Atlanta Braves.

- **2022:** Signed a six-year contract with the Los Angeles Dodgers.

- **2023:** Won his second World Series championship with the Los Angeles Dodgers and was named World Series MVP.

Key Accomplishments:

- 8-time MLB All-Star

- 2-time World Series Champion

- 1-time NL MVP

- 1-time Gold Glove Award winner

- Multiple Silver Slugger Awards

Freddie Freeman continues to be a dominant force in Major League Baseball, known for his exceptional hitting, fielding, and leadership skills.

FREDDIE FREEMAN

QUIZ

1. In what year did Freddie Freeman win the NL MVP award?

 a) 2018

b) 2020

c) 2022

d) 2024

2. What team did Freddie Freeman play for before joining the Los Angeles Dodgers?

a) New York Yankees

b) Boston Red Sox

c) Atlanta Braves

d) Chicago Cubs

3. What position does Freddie Freeman play?

a) Pitcher

b) Catcher

c) Shortstop

d) First Baseman

4. True or False: **Freddie Freeman has won multiple World Series championships.**

5. What is the name of Freddie Freeman's wife?

a) Sarah

b) Emily

c) Chelsea

d) Olivia

BASEBALL TERMS FOR

KIDS

Basic Terms:

- **Batter:** The person who tries to hit the ball.

- **Pitcher:** The person who throws the ball to the batter.

- **Catcher:** The person behind home plate who catches the ball from the pitcher.

- **Home Plate:** The rubber square where the batter stands.

- **Bases:** The four squares on the field that runners run to.

- **Infield:** The area inside the bases.

- **Outfield:** The area outside the infield.

- **Hit:** When the batter hits the ball fairly.

- **Strike:** A pitch that the batter swings at and misses, or a pitch that goes through the strike zone.

- **Ball:** A pitch that doesn't go through the strike zone.

- **Out:** When a batter or runner is eliminated.

- **Run:** A point scored when a runner crosses home plate.

- **Home Run:** A hit that allows the batter to run all the way around the bases and score.

More Fun Terms:

- **Double Play:** When two outs are made in one play.

- **Triple Play:** When three outs are made in one play.

- **Steal:** When a runner runs to the next base without the ball being hit.

- **Balk:** An illegal pitching motion that can help runners advance.

- **Wild Pitch:** A pitch that gets away from the catcher.

- **Passed Ball:** A pitch that the catcher can't catch.

Remember, baseball is a fun game, so enjoy watching and playing!

BASEBALL TACTICS

FOR KIDS

Here are some simple baseball tactics that kids can easily understand and apply:

Hitting Tactics

1. **Aim for the sweet spot:** This is the part of the bat that gives the ball the most power.

2. **Keep your eye on the ball:** Don't take your eyes off the ball until you hit it.

3. **Choke up on the bat:** This means gripping the bat higher up, which can help with control.

4. **Hit the ball where it's pitched:** Don't try to hit a home run every time. Sometimes, a single or a double is all you need.

Base Running Tactics

1. **Lead off:** When a runner stands a few steps off the base to get a better jump on the pitch.

2. **Steal a base:** When a runner runs to the next base without the ball being hit.

3. **Slide:** A way to safely reach a base, especially when a fielder is trying to tag you out.

4. **Tag up:** When a fly ball is hit, a runner on base can tag up and

advance to the next base if the

fly ball is caught.

Fielding Tactics

1. **Field the ball cleanly:** Catch the

    ball with your glove, then throw

    it accurately to the correct base.

2. **Back up other fielders:** Be

    ready to cover a base or catch a

    ball if another fielder misses it.

3. **Communicate with your**

    teammates: Talk to your

teammates to let them know where you are and what you're doing.

Pitching Tactics

1. **Mix up your pitches:** Throw different types of pitches to keep the batter guessing.

2. **Throw strikes:** Aim for the strike zone to get batters out.

3. **Use your fielders:** Work with your fielders to get outs, such as

throwing to a base to force a runner out.

Remember, these are just a few basic tactics. As you get better at baseball, you'll learn more advanced strategies. The most important thing is to have fun and enjoy the game!

Answer Key:

1. b

2. c

3. d

4. True

5. c

Made in the USA
Las Vegas, NV
17 December 2024

14552376R00046